Dedicated To:
My students

Written By: Abigail Gartland

Hello, my name is Blessed Carlo Acutis!

Blessed means that I am not quite a saint, but I will be very soon

I was born in London, England in 1991.

When I was a baby, my family moved to Milan, Italy.

When I was about seven years old, I recieved Jesus in the Eucharist for the first time.

I felt so close to the Lord and would pray in front of the tabernacle before and after every Mass!

At school. I was known to be very kind to everyone and protected others from being bullied.

On many days after school, I cared for homeless people in my city.

Like most kids, I enjoyed playing video games ...

...playing soccer...

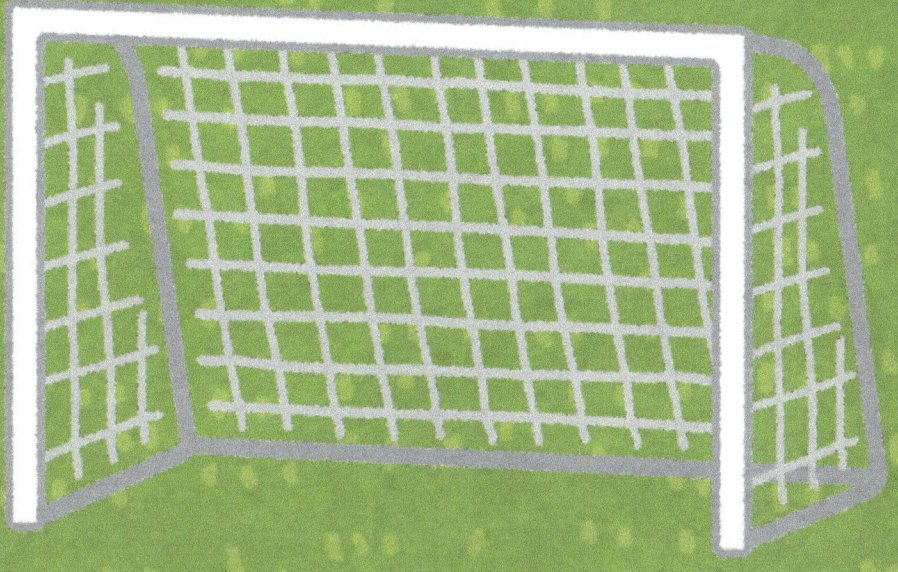

I also built my own website about the miracles of Jesus in the Eucharist.

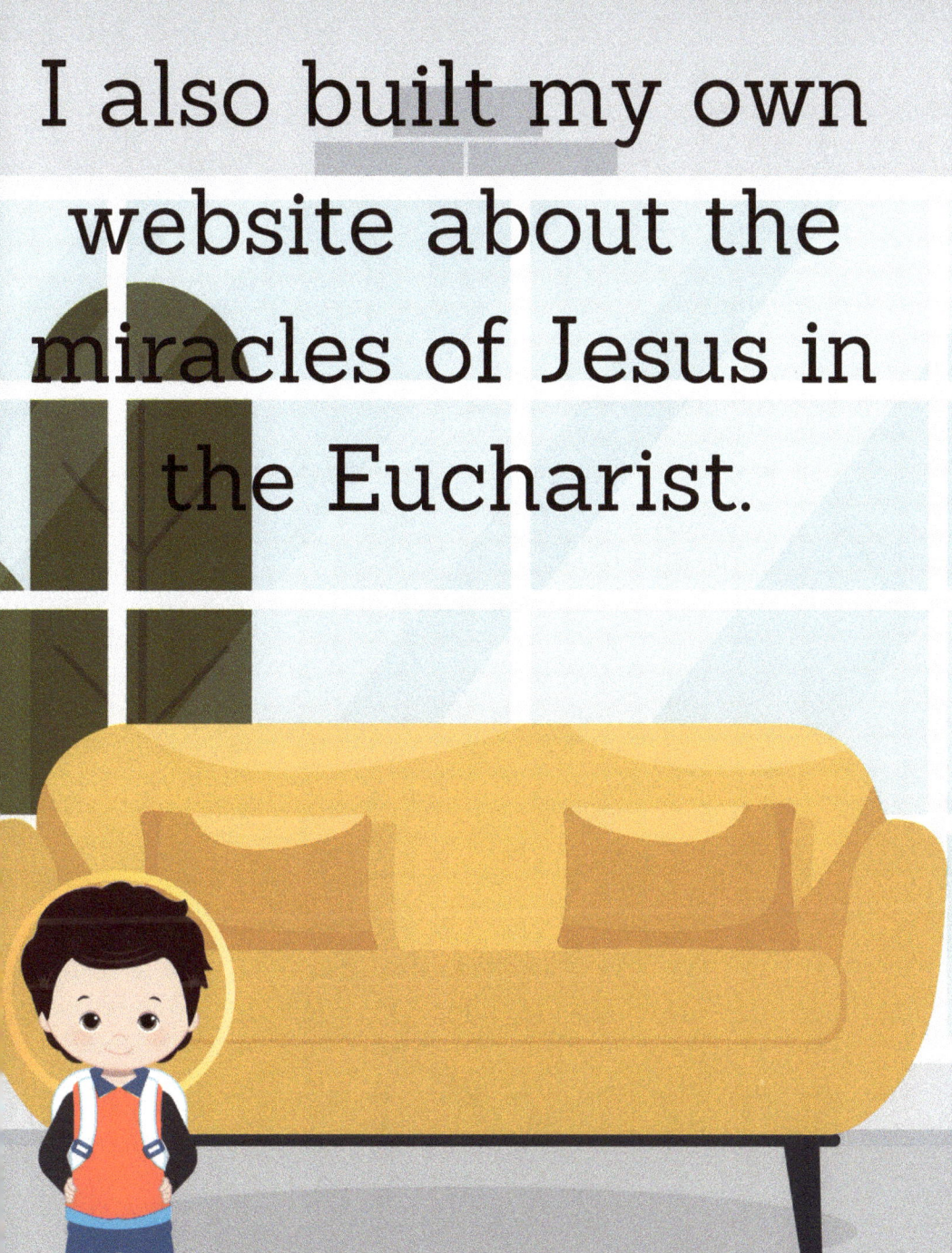

When I was a teenager, I became very sick and was diagnosed with leukemia.

On October 12, 2006, I went to Heaven to be with Jesus.

Nothing compares to the joy of being with Jesus in Heaven.

Do you want to be more like me?

I pray for you every day of your life.

Blessed Carlo Acutis, Pray for us!

Copyright:

Clipart: © PentoolPixie © LimeandKiwiDesigns
Licensed purchased: 1/10/2024

About the Author

Abigail Gartland

I love the saints and I love my faith. The idea for sharing the stories of the saints with little ones came when my dear friends were expecting their first baby. I wanted to create something as unique and special as our friendship. Each book is dedicated to very special people and groups who have enriched my faith in different ways. I am blessed to write these stories and appreciate the unending support of my family and friends. When I am not writing, I am a middle school teacher. I hope you enjoy these stories. I pray for each and every person who opens one of my books to learn more about the saints.

Abbie

www.ingramcontent.com/pod-product-compliance
Lightning Source LLC
LaVergne TN
LVHW051042070526
838201LV00067B/4894